TIPS FOR A SUCCESSFUL MARRIAGE

TIPS FOR A SUCCESSFUL MARRIAGE

Bert Witte

6th July 1996

To Natalee + Brennon
I hope it last's for ever
Love Sally + Luke
x x x x x x x x

Ideas Unlimited (Publishing)

SO YOU WANT TO GET MARRIED?

. . . And why not? There is more to life than enjoying yourself. After all, what's so special about being a free person; doing what you want, when you want, how you want, as many times as you want, with whoever you want.

Getting married and ending the marriage are both very easy, its going through what comes in between that causes the problems. It needs many years of training, a complete personality change, and a life time of responsibilities, sacrifices, and excuses.

Of course there are those who have tried marriage and swear by it. They have worked out a formula for going through it with ease, happiness and success. It is this experience and know how which is invaluable to anyone wishing to get married.

We apologise for not managing to find one such person to write this book, but we hope you will enjoy it any way.

THE FIANCÉ INTRODUCES HIS BRIDE

Paying special attention to attributes A, B, C and D. It is an unfortunate fact that attributes A, B, and C are very rarely accompanied by the attribute D-Brains. The groom will never-the-less try to convince everyone that this is in fact not the case.

A →

C

D →

B

THE SEAL OF APPROVAL

This is given first by the couple's parents, then by the Registry Office, then by society. Then it doesn't really matter any more.

THE FLORIST

Choose a responsible florist who will guarantee the appropriate bouquet for the occasion, whilst still keeping the cost within your budget.

THE CORSAGE

Choose the corsages imaginatively. Colour coding the guests according to their dreariness with the appropriate flower could ensure a smoother reception.

THE BRIDE DRESSES

Every bride to be should try to look her best on the day. But more importantly, she should try not to allow the groom to see her for weeks preceding the wedding.

THE GROOM ALSO DRESSES

A custom tailored suit is not necessary, as you can probably hire one that fits just fine. You should however allow sufficient time to master the intricacies of formal dress.

THE WEDDING DAY

The day your whole life is to change forever. Tear out the page from the calendar and treasure it. The state of this eloquant reminder should reflect the state of the marriage.

The perfect marriage

already on its sixth glass

missed 4 times

life turned upside down

another 5 pages and near misses underneath

HA HA at last!

managed to postpone it

the breadwinner has died

THE BRIDE MAKES HER APPEARANCE

It is a good idea to let the bridegroom wait for
a while, so as not to appear too over anxious.

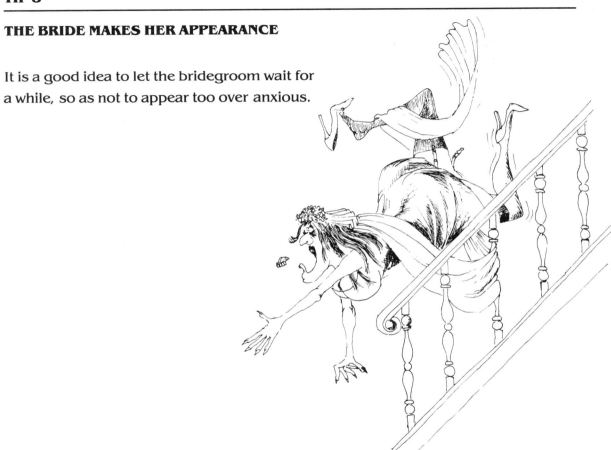

THE BEST MAN

Relying on the best man to make all the necessary arrangements is asking for trouble, particularly if he is allowed to use his initiative.

THE BRIDE'S PARENTS

Every bride should be prepared for the inevitable tears in her parent's eyes on occasions like this. It is worth a try to remind them that they are not losing a daughter but gaining a son.

THE GUEST LIST

Avoid inviting relatives you have not seen for a while. They may have changed beyond recognition.

THE TRIP TO THE WEDDING

Last minute doubts are common. A sensible bride should have an emergency plan worked out.

THE BRIDESMAIDS AND USHERS

The bridesmaids and ushers may need a little time to get to know each other, and iron out any personality clashes that may exist.

THE WAY TO THE ALTER

The use of anaesthetic is not always necessary. Sometimes a little encouragement is all that's needed.

THE RING

Always have an emergency plan worked out
incase the best man forgets the ring. It is
worth choosing a vicar who indulges in
the odd freelance side lines.

THE ALTER

If your husband to be is a man of mystery, then you must be prepared for the inevitable little surprises. . . . .And remember just because he is on first name terms with the vicar, there is no reason to get suspicious. He is probably a good Christian who goes to church regularly.

THE CEREMONY

Hiring out the additional little luxuries for the ceremony can turn out to be an expensive business. Careful timing however can eliminate unnecessary costs.

THE LITTLE SURPRISES

The reception is definately not the place to discuss the past, however recent. There is plenty of time later on for all the little things which the couple just happened to forget to tell each other before the wedding.

LOSING YOUR HEAD

Even the most upstanding pillar of society can lose his head at times; probably because of the over zealous approach to married life. If by some lucky chance, you have a lawyer in the family, pull him to one side, become his pal, because one day he will eventually play an important part in your marriage.

THE PHOTOGRAPHER

Do not be afraid to suggest one or two shots of the wedding yourself. Some photographers have their own philosophy about marriage, and always try to capture that image.

THE ENTERTAINMENT

Careful budgeting should allow for some tolerable
entertainment. You should not, under any circumstances,
opt for the cheaper alternative provided by close friends or
family.

and now for our egg joggling act; we would ask the guests to put on the aprons provided by the host. This act is very complicated and can turn out to be very messy.

DINNER TIPS

a) If you must opt for some take away, make sure the burgers and chips are unpacked before serving.
b) Avoid bachelor waiters.

A

B

MORE DINNER TIPS

Make sure that those members of the family with a somewhat dubious table manners are seated in a dark secluded area.

THE REJECTED LOVER

The rejected lover can be spotted a mile off. His unique style of concealing a severe depression is a dead give away.

THE TOASTMASTER

Remember that alcohol and the toastmaster before the toast, is a dangerous combination to be avoided; particularly if there are any skeletons in the cupboard he knows about.

SOCIALISING WITH THE GUESTS

Having gone through the ceremony like a good little boy, reward the groom by allowing him to relax and socialise with the guests.

MAKING AN EXIT

Leave the festivities gracefully; preferably without the best man. He may be one of those impossible to get rid of.

THE BILL FOR THE RECEPTION

Signing the repayment contract for the cost of the
reception can be a traumatic experience for any father.
It is worth pointing out that their investment will in the long
run, begin to show profit. The telephone bills for a start,
will once again be for more pronounceable figures.

THE PRESENTS

Some of the presents you will get may not be what you were hoping for; but do not despair — Just think of all the weddings you can go to without having to buy a present.

THE HONEYMOON

However adventurous you wish to be on your honeymoon, make sure that the transport arrangements, for the first night at least, are fairly reliable.

CROSSING THE THRESHOLD

Preserve the tradition of 'carrying the bride over the threshold' in style.

THE WEDDING NIGHT

However breathtaking you wish to be on your wedding night, you must remember that you may be expected to keep it up for the rest of your married life.

THE MOTEL

A "Do Not Disturb" sign should delay the motel staff long enough for you to clear up the debri of the night before.

MAIL ORDER WEDDING

Marriage is a life time committment. The terms of mail order shopping do not apply. So however tempting, particularly after a disastrous honeymoon, remember you <u>CAN NOT</u> exchange your new partner for a more passionate model.

THE FIRST BREAKFAST

The first breakfast may not be perfect, but at least she prepared it all by herself. So be subtle and enjoy it.

THE FIRST QUARREL

Plan the first quarrel carefully, making sure that all the unwanted wedding presents are at hand.

THE FIRST ROW

Disagreements within marriage are quite natural. Sometimes all that's needed is a little persuasion before true love and respect for the new in laws is obtained.

THE FIRST YEAR

Some newly weds are a little too over-enthusiastic to begin with. This, like all good things does not last forever, and usually dies down drastically before the year is out.

THE FIRST CHILD

It is always a most welcomed relief for the father to find out, without a shadow of a doubt, that the first child is really his.

QUIET EVENINGS AT HOME

You know your marriage is working, when you start to look forward to those quiet evenings at home.

VISITING THE IN LAWS

Visiting the in laws has its advantages. The old boy's drink cabinet for instance can be very tempting. But remember, marrying their daughter was one thing, getting too close to their other treasures may be pushing it a little.

THE NOVELTY WEARS OFF

After a few months of marriage the couple begin to go through slight hormone changes. The symptoms are, over-exhaustion in the man, and occasional head aches in the woman. A happy marriage depends on the couple's ability to synchronise these symptoms.

THE SIZE OF THE BED

Sooner or later, in any marriage the couple have to come to terms with the fact that it is not the size that matters, but rather how you use it.

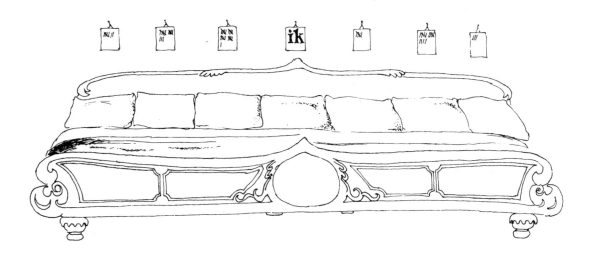

A NIGHT OUT TOGETHER

Unless you show him, your husband will not know that a night out with you can be just as fun as a night out with the boys.

AFTER A FEW YEARS OF MARRIAGE

Soon after the wedding, one partner will always begin to emerge as the dominant personality in the marriage. A sensible husband learns quickly to accept his predicament without a fight.

THE VISION OF CONTENTMENT

Sometimes the expression on one's face speaks louder than words; so don't assume that just because your loved one is silent and does not protest, he actually enjoys going shopping or is happy about doing the house work etc. Just take a good look at his face, and you'll see the truth.

HAVING AN AFFAIR

News travels fast; so if you must have an
affair, make sure that she is the silent
type. The more silent the better.

IS SHE HAVING AN AFFAIR?

There will come a time when you may suspect your wife of having an affair. Use any means to find out for sure, but do it discretely and don't let her know that you are on to her.

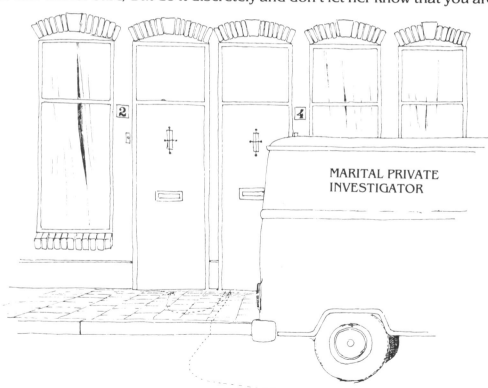

THE ALTERNATIVE EXCUSES

Going home from work a little late; shirt torn and tie hanging loose, make sure your excuse is convincing. It is sometimes worth arranging to have the odd cut and bruising implanted on you, to add a little realism to your story.

Sorry I am late dear, I was attacked by two Rottwilers and the ambulance taking me to the hospital hit a lorry . . .

MAKING UP AFTER A FIGHT

The great thing about fights in marriage is the actual making up part of it. You present her with flowers and your sincere apologies, and she in turn throws her arms around you with such passion, kissing you, loving you, and making you feel as if there never was a disagreement between you. This of course is not always the case; some ladies need a little more time to get over things.

JOINT BANK ACCOUNTS

You may find that opening a joint bank account or applying for a joint charge card could turn out to be the biggest single mistake of your life. Make sure you have a little something set aside for a rainy day.

COMPATIBILITY

There will come a time when you may begin to notice the little differences you have with your loved one. This is merely the effect of the 'love anaesthetic' wearing off, and is no cause for concern or drastic action.

THE EASY WAY OUT

Do not be tempted to try the easy way out, like joining the army, for instance; because even the army may have its pitfalls. You may be stationed too close to home, or you may be allowed visitors, or worst of all there may be someone there so much like your wife, reminding you of your wife, making life too painful to bear.

THE DIVORCE LAWYERS

The financial consequences of a divorce can be disastrous. Be prepared to divide your life's savings, property etc. into two equal halves. Each half just covering each of the two solicitor's fees.

OH WELL

. . . And if you don't succeed at first, try and try again.

TIP 56 ~~Natalee and Brennen~~

KEEP A RECORD Darren and Petrina

Monitor your marriage from the start. You may need to refer to it later on, as evidence in arguments, fights and even divorce.

	SURVIVED IT	NO. OF KISSES	GOOD LOVEMAKING	BAD LOVEMAKING	PRESENTS	VISITS TO HER MUM	VISITS TO HIS MUM	NO. OF FIGHTS
The first hour	✓							
The first day								
The first week								
The first month								
The first quarter								
The first year								
The second year								
The third year								
The fourth year								
The fifth year								
From this point on, who cares?								

OTHER TITLES AVAILABLE FROM IDEAS UNLIMITED (PUBLISHING).

Please send me:

☐ copy/copies of **"100 Chat Up Lines"** ISBN 1-871964-00-8 (128 pages A7) @ **£1.99** (postage free)
☐ copy/copies of **"Of course I Love You"** ISBN 1-871964-01-6 (96 pages A6) @ **£1.99** (postage free)
☐ copy/copies of **"The Beginners Guide to Kissing"** ISBN 1-871964-02-4 (64 pages A5) @ **£2.50** (postage free)
☐ copy/copies of **"Tips for a Successful Marriage"** ISBN 1-871964-03-2 (64 pages A5) @ **£2.50** (postage free)
☐ copy/copies of **"The Joy of Fatherhood"** ISBN 1-871964-04-0 (64 pages A5) @ **£2.50** (postage free)
☐ copy/copies of **"Office Hanky Panky"** ISBN 1-871964-05-9 (64 pages A5) @ **£2.50** (postage free)

I Have enclosed a cheque/postal order for **£**............................. made payable to Ideas Unlimited (Publishing)

Name: ....

Address: ....

Fill in the coupon and send it with your payment to: **Ideas Unlimited (Publishing) PO Box 125, Portsmouth PO1 4PP**